In the
Forest

Daphne Butler

SIMON & SCHUSTER

LONDON • SYDNEY • NEW YORK • TOKYO • SINGAPORE • TORONTO

Notes for parents and teachers

This book has a theme that threads its way through the topic. It does not aim to deal with the topic comprehensively; rather it aims to provoke thought and discussion. Each page heading makes a simple statement about the illustration which is then amplified and questioned by the text. Material in this book is particularly relevant to the following sections of the National Curriculum:

English: AT2 levels 1–3
Science: AT1 levels 1–2, AT2 levels 1–3, AT14 level 1
History: AT1 level 1 (sequencing of events)

 Remember to warn children that fungi and berries can be poisonous to humans.

TAKE ONE has been researched and compiled by Simon & Schuster Young Books. We are very grateful for the support and guidance provided by our advisory panel of professional educationalists in the course of the production.

Advisory panel:
Colin Pidgeon, Headteacher
Wheatfields Junior School, St Albans
Deirdre Walker, Deputy headteacher
Wheatfields Junior School, St Albans
Judith Clarke, Headteacher
Grove Infants School, Harpenden

British Library Cataloguing in Publication Data
Butler, Daphne, 1945–
    In the forest
    1. Forests
    I. Title II. Series
    574.52642

    ISBN 0–7500–0286–7

Series editor: Daphne Butler
Design: M&M Design Partnership
Photographs: ZEFA
except page 12 Ardea,
page 11 Heather Angel
Line drawings: Raymond Turvey

First published in Great Britain in 1990 by Simon & Schuster Young Books

Simon & Schuster Young Books
Simon & Schuster Ltd
Wolsey House, Wolsey Road
Hemel Hempstead, Herts HP2 4SS

© 1990 Simon & Schuster Young Books

All rights reserved

Printed and bound in Great Britain by BPCC Paulton Books Ltd

Contents

Forests are wild places

In a forest you may find many kinds
of plants, animals and trees.

If you have ever visited a forest,
can you remember what it was like?

Forests are different

As you walk through a forest the trees and plants will look different. They grow more strongly in some places than in others.

Sometimes the undergrowth is so thick that you can't walk through. You must go round.

9

Stop and listen

Can you hear birds singing?
Or the wind rustling in the trees?
Perhaps you can hear water
gurgling in a stream?

The sounds change as the forest
changes.

Animals in the forest

If you stay very still and quiet, you may see forest animals and birds.

The forest is their home.   They find their food there and a safe place to have their babies.

New leaves

Many forest trees have bare branches
in winter because their leaves
died in autumn.   New leaves grow
when it gets warmer in spring.

Trees that do this are called
deciduous trees.

16

Forest flowers

Between the trees, flowers grow in
the warm spring sunshine.

Later, in summer, the trees will have
many big leaves.   The ground will be shady.
Perhaps too shady for flowers.

Thick glossy leaves

Some trees have leaves all through
the year.   They are evergreen.

Do you remember seeing holly
in the forest?   Holly is evergreen.
Birds like to eat the berries in winter.

19

Forests are old

It takes a long time for trees to grow, many live for hundreds of years.

How can you tell how old a tree is? Do you think it helps to measure round the trunk?

Growth ring

22

Conifers

The oldest living thing on Earth
is a conifer.   A conifer is a tree
with needles instead of leaves and
cones instead of fruit.

There are many different conifers
in forests.   Most of them are evergreen.
They have needles on their branches
all through the year.

Keep the forest clean

You might come across rubbish left
in the forest.   It looks very ugly
and is dangerous for the animals.

The rubbish can poison the trees
and if the trees are poisoned
they may die.

Listen again

You might hear the loud buzzing of
a chain saw.   There is a forester
at work nearby.

Why do you think the forester is
cutting down trees?

Fire!

Always take care with fire.   In the forest it can be very dangerous.

In the dry summer, wind can blow fire from tree to tree.   A large part of the forest could be burnt.

What would happen to the animals that live in the forest?

29

Index